50 German Cake Dish Recipes

By: Kelly Johnson

Table of Contents

- Black Forest Cake (Schwarzwälder Kirschtorte)
- Bee Sting Cake (Bienenstich)
- German Cheesecake (Käsekuchen)
- Frankfurter Kranz
- Streuselkuchen (Crumb Cake)
- Baumkuchen (Tree Cake)
- Donauwelle (Danube Wave Cake)
- Prinzregententorte (Prince Regent Cake)
- Butterkuchen (Butter Cake)
- Mohnkuchen (Poppy Seed Cake)
- Apfelkuchen (Apple Cake)
- Rhabarberkuchen (Rhubarb Cake)
- Quarkkuchen (Quark Cake)
- Kirschtorte (Cherry Cake)
- Sandkuchen (Sponge Cake)
- Pflaumenkuchen (Plum Cake)
- Mandelkuchen (Almond Cake)
- Rotweinkuchen (Red Wine Cake)
- Haselnusskuchen (Hazelnut Cake)
- Lebkuchen (Gingerbread Cake)
- Streusel-Streifenkuchen (Streusel Strip Cake)
- Marmorkuchen (Marble Cake)
- Berliner Luft Torte (Berlin Air Cake)
- Topfkuchen (Bundt Cake)
- Linzer Torte
- Eierlikörkuchen (Egg Liqueur Cake)
- Nusskuchen (Nut Cake)
- Heidelbeerkuchen (Blueberry Cake)
- Zitronenkuchen (Lemon Cake)
- Stollen (Christmas Cake)
- Gugelhupf (Bundt Cake)
- Kirsch-Streuselkuchen (Cherry Crumb Cake)
- Zwetschgendatschi (Bavarian Plum Cake)
- Sahnetorte (Cream Cake)
- Weihnachtsstollen (Christmas Stollen)

- Schneewittchenkuchen (Snow White Cake)
- Joghurtkuchen (Yogurt Cake)
- Schmandkuchen (Sour Cream Cake)
- Erdbeerkuchen (Strawberry Cake)
- Rahmkuchen (Cream Cake)
- Karamellkuchen (Caramel Cake)
- Windbeuteltorte (Cream Puff Cake)
- Dominosteinkuchen (Domino Cake)
- Heidelbeer-Sahnetorte (Blueberry Cream Cake)
- Zwetschgenkuchen mit Zimt (Cinnamon Plum Cake)
- Vanillekuchen (Vanilla Cake)
- Holunderblütenkuchen (Elderflower Cake)
- Marmor-Sahnetorte (Marble Cream Cake)
- Schokoladenkuchen (Chocolate Cake)
- Frankfurter Apfelweinkuchen (Frankfurt Apple Wine Cake)

Black Forest Cake (Schwarzwälder Kirschtorte)

Ingredients:

For the Cake:

- 1 ½ cups flour
- ½ cup cocoa powder
- 1 teaspoon baking powder
- 1 teaspoon baking soda
- 1 cup sugar
- ½ cup butter
- 3 eggs
- 1 teaspoon vanilla
- ¾ cup buttermilk

For the Filling & Topping:

- 2 cups cherries (fresh or canned)
- ¼ cup Kirsch (cherry brandy)
- 2 cups heavy cream
- ¼ cup powdered sugar
- Chocolate shavings

Instructions:

1. Preheat oven to 350°F (175°C). Grease two cake pans.
2. Beat butter and sugar, then add eggs and vanilla.
3. Mix in dry ingredients and buttermilk.
4. Divide into pans and bake for 30 minutes. Cool completely.
5. Soak cherries in Kirsch for 15 minutes.
6. Whip cream with powdered sugar.
7. Layer cakes with cherries and whipped cream. Top with chocolate shavings.

Bee Sting Cake (Bienenstich)

Ingredients:

For the Dough:

- 2 cups flour
- ½ cup warm milk
- ¼ cup sugar
- 1 packet yeast
- 2 eggs
- ¼ cup butter

For the Topping:

- ½ cup butter
- ½ cup honey
- ½ cup sliced almonds

For the Filling:

- 2 cups milk
- ½ cup sugar
- 1 packet vanilla pudding mix
- ½ cup butter

Instructions:

1. Mix yeast, warm milk, and sugar. Let sit for 10 minutes.
2. Add eggs, butter, and flour, knead, and let rise for 1 hour.
3. For topping, melt butter and honey, then add almonds.
4. Roll dough into a pan, spread almond topping, and bake at 350°F (175°C) for 25 minutes.
5. Prepare pudding, cool, then mix with butter.
6. Slice cake in half and fill with cream.

German Cheesecake (Käsekuchen)

Ingredients:

For the Crust:

- 1 ½ cups flour
- ½ cup butter
- ¼ cup sugar
- 1 egg

For the Filling:

- 2 cups quark or ricotta cheese
- 1 cup sugar
- 3 eggs
- 1 teaspoon vanilla
- ½ cup heavy cream

Instructions:

1. Preheat oven to 350°F (175°C). Mix crust ingredients and press into a pan.
2. Beat filling ingredients until smooth.
3. Pour over crust and bake for 50 minutes.
4. Cool and chill before serving.

Frankfurter Kranz

Ingredients:

For the Cake:

- 2 cups flour
- 1 teaspoon baking powder
- 1 cup butter
- 1 cup sugar
- 4 eggs
- 1 teaspoon vanilla

For the Filling & Topping:

- 1 cup butter
- 1 ½ cups powdered sugar
- ½ cup raspberry jam
- Caramelized nuts

Instructions:

1. Preheat oven to 350°F (175°C).
2. Beat butter and sugar, then add eggs and vanilla.
3. Mix in flour and baking powder. Bake for 35 minutes.
4. Slice into layers and fill with buttercream and jam.
5. Cover with buttercream and sprinkle with nuts.

Streuselkuchen (Crumb Cake)

Ingredients:

For the Dough:

- 2 cups flour
- ½ cup warm milk
- ¼ cup sugar
- 1 packet yeast
- ¼ cup butter

For the Streusel Topping:

- ½ cup flour
- ¼ cup sugar
- ¼ cup butter

Instructions:

1. Mix yeast, warm milk, and sugar. Let sit for 10 minutes.
2. Add butter and flour, knead, and let rise for 1 hour.
3. Spread dough in a pan.
4. Mix streusel ingredients until crumbly and sprinkle over dough.
5. Bake at 350°F (175°C) for 25 minutes.

Baumkuchen (Tree Cake)

Ingredients:

- 1 cup butter
- 1 cup sugar
- 6 eggs
- 1 teaspoon vanilla
- 1 ½ cups flour
- ½ cup cornstarch

Instructions:

1. Preheat oven to 400°F (200°C).
2. Beat butter and sugar, then add eggs one at a time.
3. Mix in flour and cornstarch.
4. Spread a thin layer in a pan and bake until golden. Repeat in layers.
5. Serve once all layers are baked.

Donauwelle (Danube Wave Cake)

Ingredients:

For the Cake:

- 1 cup butter
- 1 cup sugar
- 4 eggs
- 2 cups flour
- 1 teaspoon baking powder
- ½ cup cocoa powder

For the Topping:

- 1 ½ cups cherries
- 2 cups vanilla pudding
- 1 ½ cups melted chocolate

Instructions:

1. Preheat oven to 350°F (175°C).
2. Beat butter and sugar, then add eggs.
3. Mix in flour and baking powder.
4. Divide batter in half; mix cocoa into one half.
5. Spread plain batter in a pan, then chocolate batter.
6. Add cherries and bake for 30 minutes.
7. Spread pudding over cooled cake, then top with melted chocolate.

Prinzregententorte (Prince Regent Cake)

Ingredients:

- 1 ½ cups flour
- 1 cup sugar
- 4 eggs
- ½ cup butter
- 1 teaspoon vanilla
- 2 cups chocolate buttercream

Instructions:

1. Preheat oven to 350°F (175°C).
2. Beat butter and sugar, then add eggs and vanilla.
3. Mix in flour.
4. Divide into 6 thin layers and bake for 10 minutes each.
5. Stack layers with chocolate buttercream.

Butterkuchen (Butter Cake)

Ingredients:

- 2 cups flour
- ½ cup warm milk
- ¼ cup sugar
- 1 packet yeast
- ¼ cup butter

Instructions:

1. Mix yeast, warm milk, and sugar. Let sit for 10 minutes.
2. Add butter and flour, knead, and let rise for 1 hour.
3. Spread in a pan, make dimples, and add extra butter and sugar.
4. Bake at 350°F (175°C) for 25 minutes.

Mohnkuchen (Poppy Seed Cake)

Ingredients:

For the Dough:

- 2 cups flour
- ½ cup warm milk
- ¼ cup sugar
- 1 packet yeast

For the Filling:

- 1 cup ground poppy seeds
- ½ cup sugar
- 1 cup milk

Instructions:

1. Mix yeast, warm milk, and sugar. Let sit for 10 minutes.
2. Add flour and knead. Let rise for 1 hour.
3. For filling, mix poppy seeds with sugar and milk.
4. Roll out dough, spread filling, and bake at 350°F (175°C) for 30 minutes.

Apfelkuchen (Apple Cake)

Ingredients:

- 2 cups flour
- 1 cup sugar
- ½ cup butter
- 3 eggs
- 2 teaspoons baking powder
- 3 apples (sliced)

Instructions:

1. Preheat oven to 350°F (175°C).
2. Beat butter and sugar, then add eggs.
3. Mix in flour and baking powder.
4. Fold in apple slices and bake for 40 minutes.

Rhabarberkuchen (Rhubarb Cake)

Ingredients:

For the Cake:

- 2 cups flour
- 1 teaspoon baking powder
- ½ cup butter
- ¾ cup sugar
- 3 eggs
- ½ cup milk
- 3 cups rhubarb, chopped

For the Topping:

- ¼ cup sugar
- 1 teaspoon cinnamon

Instructions:

1. Preheat oven to 350°F (175°C).
2. Beat butter and sugar, then add eggs.
3. Mix in flour, baking powder, and milk.
4. Spread batter in a pan and top with rhubarb.
5. Sprinkle with cinnamon and sugar.
6. Bake for 35-40 minutes.

Quarkkuchen (Quark Cake)

Ingredients:

For the Crust:

- 1 ½ cups flour
- ½ cup butter
- ¼ cup sugar
- 1 egg

For the Filling:

- 2 cups quark
- 1 cup sugar
- 3 eggs
- ½ cup heavy cream
- 1 teaspoon vanilla

Instructions:

1. Preheat oven to 350°F (175°C).
2. Mix crust ingredients and press into a pan.
3. Beat filling ingredients until smooth and pour over crust.
4. Bake for 50 minutes.
5. Cool before serving.

Kirschtorte (Cherry Cake)

Ingredients:

- 2 cups flour
- 1 teaspoon baking powder
- ½ cup butter
- ¾ cup sugar
- 3 eggs
- ½ cup milk
- 2 cups cherries (pitted)

Instructions:

1. Preheat oven to 350°F (175°C).
2. Beat butter and sugar, then add eggs.
3. Mix in flour, baking powder, and milk.
4. Fold in cherries and pour into a greased pan.
5. Bake for 40 minutes.

Sandkuchen (Sponge Cake)

Ingredients:

- 2 cups flour
- 1 teaspoon baking powder
- 1 cup butter
- 1 cup sugar
- 4 eggs
- 1 teaspoon vanilla
- ½ cup milk

Instructions:

1. Preheat oven to 350°F (175°C).
2. Beat butter and sugar, then add eggs one at a time.
3. Mix in flour, baking powder, vanilla, and milk.
4. Pour into a loaf pan and bake for 45 minutes.

Pflaumenkuchen (Plum Cake)

Ingredients:

For the Dough:

- 2 cups flour
- ½ cup warm milk
- ¼ cup sugar
- 1 packet yeast
- ¼ cup butter

For the Topping:

- 2 cups plums (sliced)
- ¼ cup sugar
- 1 teaspoon cinnamon

Instructions:

1. Mix yeast, warm milk, and sugar. Let sit for 10 minutes.
2. Add flour and butter, knead, and let rise for 1 hour.
3. Roll out dough and place in a pan.
4. Arrange plums on top, sprinkle with cinnamon and sugar.
5. Bake at 350°F (175°C) for 30 minutes.

Mandelkuchen (Almond Cake)

Ingredients:

- 1 ½ cups flour
- 1 cup sugar
- ½ cup butter
- 3 eggs
- 1 teaspoon baking powder
- ½ cup ground almonds
- ½ cup milk
- ¼ cup sliced almonds (for topping)

Instructions:

1. Preheat oven to 350°F (175°C).
2. Beat butter and sugar, then add eggs.
3. Mix in flour, baking powder, ground almonds, and milk.
4. Pour into a pan, sprinkle with sliced almonds.
5. Bake for 40 minutes.

Rotweinkuchen (Red Wine Cake)

Ingredients:

- 2 cups flour
- 1 teaspoon baking powder
- 1 cup sugar
- ½ cup butter
- 4 eggs
- 1 cup red wine
- ¼ cup cocoa powder
- 1 teaspoon cinnamon

Instructions:

1. Preheat oven to 350°F (175°C).
2. Beat butter and sugar, then add eggs.
3. Mix in flour, baking powder, cocoa, cinnamon, and red wine.
4. Pour into a pan and bake for 40 minutes.

Haselnusskuchen (Hazelnut Cake)

Ingredients:

- 1 ½ cups flour
- 1 cup ground hazelnuts
- 1 cup sugar
- ½ cup butter
- 3 eggs
- 1 teaspoon baking powder
- ½ cup milk

Instructions:

1. Preheat oven to 350°F (175°C).
2. Beat butter and sugar, then add eggs.
3. Mix in flour, hazelnuts, baking powder, and milk.
4. Pour into a pan and bake for 40 minutes.

Lebkuchen (Gingerbread Cake)

Ingredients:

- 2 cups flour
- ½ cup sugar
- ½ cup honey
- 1 egg
- 1 teaspoon baking powder
- 1 teaspoon cinnamon
- ½ teaspoon cloves
- ½ teaspoon nutmeg
- ½ teaspoon ginger

Instructions:

1. Preheat oven to 350°F (175°C).
2. Beat honey, sugar, and egg.
3. Mix in flour, baking powder, and spices.
4. Pour into a pan and bake for 30 minutes.

Streusel-Streifenkuchen (Streusel Strip Cake)

Ingredients:

For the Dough:

- 2 ½ cups flour
- ½ cup sugar
- 1 packet (7g) yeast
- ½ cup warm milk
- ¼ cup butter
- 1 egg

For the Streusel Topping:

- 1 cup flour
- ½ cup sugar
- ½ cup butter

Instructions:

1. Mix yeast, warm milk, and sugar. Let sit for 10 minutes.
2. Add flour, butter, and egg, knead into a dough. Let rise for 1 hour.
3. Roll out the dough into strips and place on a baking sheet.
4. Mix streusel topping ingredients until crumbly and sprinkle over dough.
5. Bake at 350°F (175°C) for 25 minutes.

Marmorkuchen (Marble Cake)

Ingredients:

- 2 ½ cups flour
- 1 teaspoon baking powder
- 1 cup butter
- 1 cup sugar
- 4 eggs
- ½ cup milk
- ¼ cup cocoa powder

Instructions:

1. Preheat oven to 350°F (175°C).
2. Beat butter and sugar, then add eggs.
3. Mix in flour, baking powder, and milk.
4. Divide batter in half; mix cocoa powder into one half.
5. Pour both batters alternately into a bundt pan and swirl with a fork.
6. Bake for 50 minutes.

Berliner Luft Torte (Berlin Air Cake)

Ingredients:

For the Cake:

- 4 egg whites
- 1 cup sugar
- 1 teaspoon vanilla
- 1 cup ground almonds

For the Filling:

- 1 cup heavy cream
- ¼ cup sugar
- 1 teaspoon lemon zest

Instructions:

1. Preheat oven to 300°F (150°C).
2. Beat egg whites until stiff, then add sugar and vanilla.
3. Fold in ground almonds and pour into a cake pan.
4. Bake for 30 minutes.
5. Beat cream with sugar and lemon zest, then spread between cake layers.

Topfkuchen (Bundt Cake)

Ingredients:

- 2 ½ cups flour
- 1 teaspoon baking powder
- 1 cup butter
- 1 cup sugar
- 4 eggs
- ½ cup milk
- 1 teaspoon vanilla

Instructions:

1. Preheat oven to 350°F (175°C).
2. Beat butter and sugar, then add eggs.
3. Mix in flour, baking powder, milk, and vanilla.
4. Pour into a bundt pan and bake for 50 minutes.

Linzer Torte

Ingredients:

- 1 ½ cups flour
- 1 cup ground hazelnuts
- ½ cup sugar
- ½ teaspoon cinnamon
- ½ teaspoon cloves
- ½ cup butter
- 1 egg
- ½ cup raspberry jam

Instructions:

1. Preheat oven to 350°F (175°C).
2. Mix flour, nuts, sugar, and spices.
3. Add butter and egg, knead into a dough.
4. Press ¾ of dough into a tart pan, spread with jam.
5. Roll out remaining dough into strips and create a lattice.
6. Bake for 35 minutes.

Eierlikörkuchen (Egg Liqueur Cake)

Ingredients:

- 2 ½ cups flour
- 1 teaspoon baking powder
- 1 cup sugar
- 1 cup butter
- 4 eggs
- ½ cup egg liqueur (e.g., Advocaat)

Instructions:

1. Preheat oven to 350°F (175°C).
2. Beat butter and sugar, then add eggs.
3. Mix in flour, baking powder, and egg liqueur.
4. Pour into a bundt pan and bake for 50 minutes.

Nusskuchen (Nut Cake)

Ingredients:

- 2 cups flour
- 1 teaspoon baking powder
- 1 cup ground nuts (hazelnuts or walnuts)
- 1 cup sugar
- ½ cup butter
- 3 eggs
- ½ cup milk

Instructions:

1. Preheat oven to 350°F (175°C).
2. Beat butter and sugar, then add eggs.
3. Mix in flour, baking powder, nuts, and milk.
4. Pour into a loaf pan and bake for 40 minutes.

Heidelbeerkuchen (Blueberry Cake)

Ingredients:

- 2 cups flour
- 1 teaspoon baking powder
- 1 cup sugar
- ½ cup butter
- 3 eggs
- ½ cup milk
- 1 ½ cups blueberries

Instructions:

1. Preheat oven to 350°F (175°C).
2. Beat butter and sugar, then add eggs.
3. Mix in flour, baking powder, and milk.
4. Fold in blueberries and pour into a pan.
5. Bake for 40 minutes.

Zitronenkuchen (Lemon Cake)

Ingredients:

- 2 cups flour
- 1 teaspoon baking powder
- 1 cup sugar
- ½ cup butter
- 3 eggs
- ½ cup milk
- 2 tablespoons lemon juice
- 1 teaspoon lemon zest

Instructions:

1. Preheat oven to 350°F (175°C).
2. Beat butter and sugar, then add eggs.
3. Mix in flour, baking powder, milk, lemon juice, and zest.
4. Pour into a loaf pan and bake for 40 minutes.

Stollen (Christmas Cake)

Ingredients:

- 4 cups flour
- 1 packet (7g) yeast
- ½ cup warm milk
- ½ cup sugar
- ½ cup butter
- 1 egg
- ½ teaspoon cinnamon
- ½ teaspoon nutmeg
- ½ cup raisins
- ½ cup chopped almonds
- ½ cup candied citrus peel

Instructions:

1. Mix yeast, warm milk, and sugar. Let sit for 10 minutes.
2. Add flour, butter, egg, and spices. Knead into a dough.
3. Mix in raisins, almonds, and citrus peel.
4. Shape into a loaf and let rise for 1 hour.
5. Bake at 350°F (175°C) for 45 minutes.

Gugelhupf (Bundt Cake)

Ingredients:

- 2 ½ cups flour
- 1 teaspoon baking powder
- 1 cup butter
- 1 cup sugar
- 4 eggs
- ½ cup milk
- 1 teaspoon vanilla extract
- ½ cup chopped almonds (optional)
- ½ cup raisins (optional)
- Powdered sugar for dusting

Instructions:

1. Preheat oven to 350°F (175°C).
2. Grease a Bundt pan and dust with flour.
3. Beat butter and sugar until fluffy, then add eggs one at a time.
4. Mix in flour, baking powder, and milk.
5. Fold in almonds and raisins if using.
6. Pour into the pan and bake for 50-60 minutes.
7. Let cool, then dust with powdered sugar.

Kirsch-Streuselkuchen (Cherry Crumb Cake)

Ingredients:

For the Cake:

- 2 cups flour
- 1 teaspoon baking powder
- ½ cup butter
- ½ cup sugar
- 2 eggs
- ½ cup milk
- 2 cups pitted cherries

For the Streusel Topping:

- 1 cup flour
- ½ cup sugar
- ½ cup butter

Instructions:

1. Preheat oven to 350°F (175°C).
2. Beat butter and sugar, then add eggs.
3. Mix in flour, baking powder, and milk. Pour into a greased pan.
4. Spread cherries evenly on top.
5. Mix streusel ingredients into crumbs and sprinkle over the cherries.
6. Bake for 40-45 minutes.

Zwetschgendatschi (Bavarian Plum Cake)

Ingredients:

- 2 ½ cups flour
- ½ cup butter
- ½ cup sugar
- 1 egg
- 1 teaspoon vanilla extract
- ½ teaspoon baking powder
- 2 lbs fresh plums, halved and pitted
- ½ teaspoon cinnamon
- 2 tablespoons sugar (for topping)

Instructions:

1. Preheat oven to 350°F (175°C).
2. Mix flour, butter, sugar, egg, vanilla, and baking powder into a dough.
3. Press into a baking pan.
4. Arrange plums in rows, cut side up.
5. Sprinkle with cinnamon and sugar.
6. Bake for 40-45 minutes.

Sahnetorte (Cream Cake)

Ingredients:

For the Cake:

- 4 eggs
- 1 cup sugar
- 1 cup flour
- 1 teaspoon baking powder

For the Filling:

- 2 cups heavy cream
- ¼ cup powdered sugar
- 1 teaspoon vanilla extract

Instructions:

1. Preheat oven to 350°F (175°C).
2. Beat eggs and sugar until fluffy.
3. Gently fold in flour and baking powder.
4. Pour into a springform pan and bake for 25-30 minutes.
5. Let cool, then slice in half horizontally.
6. Whip cream with powdered sugar and vanilla.
7. Spread cream between layers and on top.
8. Refrigerate for 1 hour before serving.

Weihnachtsstollen (Christmas Stollen)

Ingredients:

- 4 cups flour
- 1 packet (7g) yeast
- ½ cup warm milk
- ½ cup sugar
- ½ cup butter
- 1 egg
- ½ teaspoon cinnamon
- ½ teaspoon nutmeg
- ½ cup raisins
- ½ cup chopped almonds
- ½ cup candied citrus peel
- 2 tablespoons rum
- Powdered sugar for dusting

Instructions:

1. Soak raisins in rum overnight.
2. Mix yeast, warm milk, and sugar. Let sit for 10 minutes.
3. Add flour, butter, egg, and spices. Knead into a dough.
4. Mix in raisins, almonds, and citrus peel.
5. Shape into a loaf and let rise for 1 hour.
6. Bake at 350°F (175°C) for 45 minutes.
7. Dust with powdered sugar while warm.

Schneewittchenkuchen (Snow White Cake)

Ingredients:

- 2 cups flour
- 1 teaspoon baking powder
- 1 cup sugar
- ½ cup butter
- 3 eggs
- ½ cup milk
- 2 cups cherries
- 2 cups whipped cream

Instructions:

1. Preheat oven to 350°F (175°C).
2. Beat butter and sugar, then add eggs.
3. Mix in flour, baking powder, and milk.
4. Pour into a greased pan and bake for 30-35 minutes.
5. Let cool, then spread whipped cream and top with cherries.

Joghurtkuchen (Yogurt Cake)

Ingredients:

- 2 cups flour
- 1 teaspoon baking powder
- 1 cup plain yogurt
- ½ cup sugar
- ½ cup vegetable oil
- 3 eggs
- 1 teaspoon vanilla

Instructions:

1. Preheat oven to 350°F (175°C).
2. Beat sugar and eggs, then mix in yogurt and oil.
3. Add flour, baking powder, and vanilla.
4. Pour into a greased loaf pan and bake for 40 minutes.

Schmandkuchen (Sour Cream Cake)

Ingredients:

For the Crust:

- 2 cups flour
- ½ cup butter
- ½ cup sugar
- 1 egg

For the Filling:

- 2 cups sour cream
- ½ cup sugar
- 1 teaspoon vanilla
- 2 eggs

Instructions:

1. Preheat oven to 350°F (175°C).
2. Mix crust ingredients, press into a baking pan.
3. Beat filling ingredients and pour over the crust.
4. Bake for 35-40 minutes.

Erdbeerkuchen (Strawberry Cake)

Ingredients:

- 2 cups flour
- 1 teaspoon baking powder
- 1 cup sugar
- ½ cup butter
- 3 eggs
- ½ cup milk
- 2 cups fresh strawberries
- 1 cup whipped cream

Instructions:

1. Preheat oven to 350°F (175°C).
2. Beat butter and sugar, then add eggs.
3. Mix in flour, baking powder, and milk.
4. Pour into a greased pan and bake for 30 minutes.
5. Let cool, spread with whipped cream, and top with strawberries.

Rahmkuchen (Cream Cake)

Ingredients:

For the Crust:

- 2 cups flour
- ½ cup butter
- ½ cup sugar
- 1 egg

For the Filling:

- 2 cups heavy cream
- ½ cup sugar
- 1 teaspoon vanilla
- 2 eggs

Instructions:

1. Preheat oven to 350°F (175°C).
2. Mix crust ingredients, press into a baking pan.
3. Beat filling ingredients and pour over the crust.
4. Bake for 35-40 minutes.

Karamellkuchen (Caramel Cake)

Ingredients:

For the Cake:

- 2 cups flour
- 1 cup sugar
- ½ cup butter, softened
- 3 eggs
- 1 teaspoon vanilla extract
- ½ cup milk
- 1 teaspoon baking powder
- ½ teaspoon salt

For the Caramel Sauce:

- 1 cup sugar
- ½ cup heavy cream
- ¼ cup butter
- ½ teaspoon sea salt

Instructions:

1. **Preheat oven** to 350°F (175°C) and grease a cake pan.
2. **Make the cake batter:** Beat butter and sugar until fluffy, then add eggs one at a time. Mix in vanilla.
3. **Add dry ingredients:** Sift together flour, baking powder, and salt. Add to the mixture, alternating with milk.
4. **Bake:** Pour into the pan and bake for 30-35 minutes. Let cool.
5. **Prepare caramel sauce:** Melt sugar in a saucepan over medium heat until amber in color. Stir in butter, then slowly add heavy cream while whisking. Add salt and let cool slightly.
6. **Assemble:** Drizzle caramel over the cake before serving.

Windbeuteltorte (Cream Puff Cake)

Ingredients:

For the Cream Puff Base:

- 1 cup water
- ½ cup butter
- 1 cup flour
- 4 eggs
- ¼ teaspoon salt

For the Filling:

- 2 cups heavy cream
- ¼ cup powdered sugar
- 1 teaspoon vanilla extract

For the Topping:

- ½ cup melted chocolate

Instructions:

1. **Preheat oven** to 375°F (190°C) and grease a springform pan.
2. **Make the dough:** Boil water and butter in a saucepan. Remove from heat and stir in flour and salt.
3. **Add eggs:** Beat in eggs one at a time until smooth.
4. **Bake the base:** Spread dough in the pan and bake for 25-30 minutes. Let cool.
5. **Make filling:** Whip heavy cream with powdered sugar and vanilla.
6. **Assemble:** Spread whipped cream over the baked base. Drizzle with melted chocolate before serving.

Dominosteinkuchen (Domino Cake)

Ingredients:

For the Cake Base:

- 2 cups flour
- 1 teaspoon baking powder
- ½ cup sugar
- ½ cup butter
- 3 eggs
- ½ cup milk

For the Layers:

- ½ cup apricot jam
- ½ cup marzipan
- ½ cup dark chocolate, melted

Instructions:

1. **Preheat oven** to 350°F (175°C) and grease a baking pan.
2. **Make cake batter:** Beat butter and sugar until fluffy, then add eggs. Mix in flour, baking powder, and milk.
3. **Bake:** Pour into the pan and bake for 25-30 minutes. Let cool.
4. **Assemble layers:** Spread apricot jam over the cake. Roll out marzipan and place on top.
5. **Coat with chocolate:** Pour melted dark chocolate over the cake and let set before cutting into squares.

Heidelbeer-Sahnetorte (Blueberry Cream Cake)

Ingredients:

For the Sponge Cake:

- 4 eggs
- ¾ cup sugar
- 1 cup flour
- 1 teaspoon baking powder

For the Filling:

- 2 cups heavy cream
- ¼ cup powdered sugar
- 1 teaspoon vanilla extract
- 1 cup fresh blueberries

For the Topping:

- ½ cup blueberry jam
- ½ cup fresh blueberries

Instructions:

1. **Preheat oven** to 350°F (175°C) and grease a cake pan.
2. **Make sponge cake:** Beat eggs and sugar until fluffy. Fold in flour and baking powder.
3. **Bake:** Pour into the pan and bake for 20-25 minutes. Let cool.
4. **Prepare filling:** Whip heavy cream with powdered sugar and vanilla until stiff peaks form.
5. **Assemble cake:** Slice cake in half. Spread whipped cream and blueberries on one layer, then place the second layer on top.
6. **Add topping:** Warm blueberry jam slightly and spread over the top. Decorate with fresh blueberries.

Zwetschgenkuchen mit Zimt (Cinnamon Plum Cake)

Ingredients:

For the Dough:

- 2 cups flour
- ½ cup butter
- ½ cup sugar
- 1 egg
- 1 teaspoon baking powder
- ½ teaspoon salt

For the Topping:

- 1 ½ lbs fresh plums, halved and pitted
- ½ cup sugar
- 1 teaspoon cinnamon
- ¼ cup sliced almonds (optional)

Instructions:

1. Preheat oven to 350°F (175°C).
2. Mix flour, sugar, salt, and baking powder. Cut in butter, then add the egg to form a dough.
3. Press the dough into a greased round cake pan.
4. Arrange plums on top and sprinkle with cinnamon and sugar. Add almonds if desired.
5. Bake for 35-40 minutes until golden brown.

Vanillekuchen (Vanilla Cake)

Ingredients:

- 2 cups flour
- 1 cup sugar
- ½ cup butter
- 3 eggs
- 1 teaspoon vanilla extract
- 1 teaspoon baking powder
- ½ cup milk

Instructions:

1. Preheat oven to 350°F (175°C). Grease a cake pan.
2. Beat butter and sugar until fluffy, then add eggs and vanilla.
3. Mix in flour and baking powder, alternating with milk.
4. Pour into the pan and bake for 30-35 minutes until a toothpick comes out clean.

Holunderblütenkuchen (Elderflower Cake)

Ingredients:

- 2 cups flour
- 1 teaspoon baking powder
- ½ cup butter
- ¾ cup sugar
- 3 eggs
- ½ cup elderflower syrup
- ½ cup milk

For the Glaze:

- ½ cup powdered sugar
- 2 tablespoons elderflower syrup

Instructions:

1. Preheat oven to 350°F (175°C).
2. Beat butter and sugar, then add eggs one at a time.
3. Mix in flour and baking powder, alternating with elderflower syrup and milk.
4. Pour into a cake pan and bake for 30-35 minutes.
5. Mix powdered sugar with elderflower syrup and drizzle over the cooled cake.

Marmor-Sahnetorte (Marble Cream Cake)

Ingredients:

For the Cake:

- 2 cups flour
- 1 cup sugar
- ½ cup butter
- 3 eggs
- 1 teaspoon vanilla extract
- ½ cup milk
- 2 tablespoons cocoa powder

For the Cream Filling:

- 2 cups heavy cream
- ¼ cup powdered sugar
- 1 teaspoon vanilla extract

Instructions:

1. Preheat oven to 350°F (175°C).
2. Beat butter and sugar, then add eggs and vanilla. Mix in flour and baking powder, alternating with milk.
3. Divide the batter in half. Mix cocoa powder into one half.
4. Swirl both batters together in a greased cake pan and bake for 30-35 minutes.
5. Whip heavy cream with powdered sugar and vanilla. Slice cake in half and spread cream in between.

Schokoladenkuchen (Chocolate Cake)

Ingredients:

- 1 ½ cups flour
- ¾ cup sugar
- ½ cup butter
- ½ cup cocoa powder
- 3 eggs
- 1 teaspoon vanilla extract
- ½ teaspoon baking powder
- ½ cup milk

Instructions:

1. Preheat oven to 350°F (175°C).
2. Beat butter and sugar until fluffy, then add eggs and vanilla.
3. Mix in flour, cocoa, and baking powder, alternating with milk.
4. Pour into a cake pan and bake for 30-35 minutes.

Frankfurter Apfelweinkuchen (Frankfurt Apple Wine Cake)

Ingredients:

For the Crust:

- 2 cups flour
- ½ cup butter
- ½ cup sugar
- 1 egg
- 1 teaspoon baking powder

For the Filling:

- 4 apples, peeled and sliced
- 1 cup apple wine (or apple juice)
- ½ cup sugar
- 1 teaspoon cinnamon
- 1 cup sour cream
- 2 eggs

Instructions:

1. Preheat oven to 350°F (175°C).
2. Mix crust ingredients and press into a greased springform pan.
3. Arrange apples on top and sprinkle with sugar and cinnamon.
4. Mix apple wine, sour cream, and eggs, then pour over the apples.
5. Bake for 40-45 minutes.

www.ingramcontent.com/pod-product-compliance
Lightning Source LLC
LaVergne TN
LVHW081338060526
838201LV00055B/2713